Once upon a Time in Space

In my bed it seems so odd
To think that once, except for God,

Nothing was: no trees, no men,
No animals or oxygen.

And even more—for what it's worth—
Once there wasn't even Earth,

Or Venus, Jupiter, or Mars;
The sky lacked all its salty stars,

Which means, of course, no glowing sun
To warm or brighten anyone.

(In fact, how could there be a fuel
Before God built a molecule?)

Yet God was there as "Father," "Son,"
And "Holy Spirit"—three in One.

Then once upon a time in space
God planned and put a world in place,

One carefully laid out just so,
Just as I am from head to toe.

It staggers my imagination
To consider all creation,

And that time when God was there
And every space in space was bare.

How can I ever sleep in bed
When such things jangle in my head?

John 1:1-3
Psalm 90:1-2
Genesis 1

1

A
Pillar of Pepper
and
other Bible
nursery rhymes

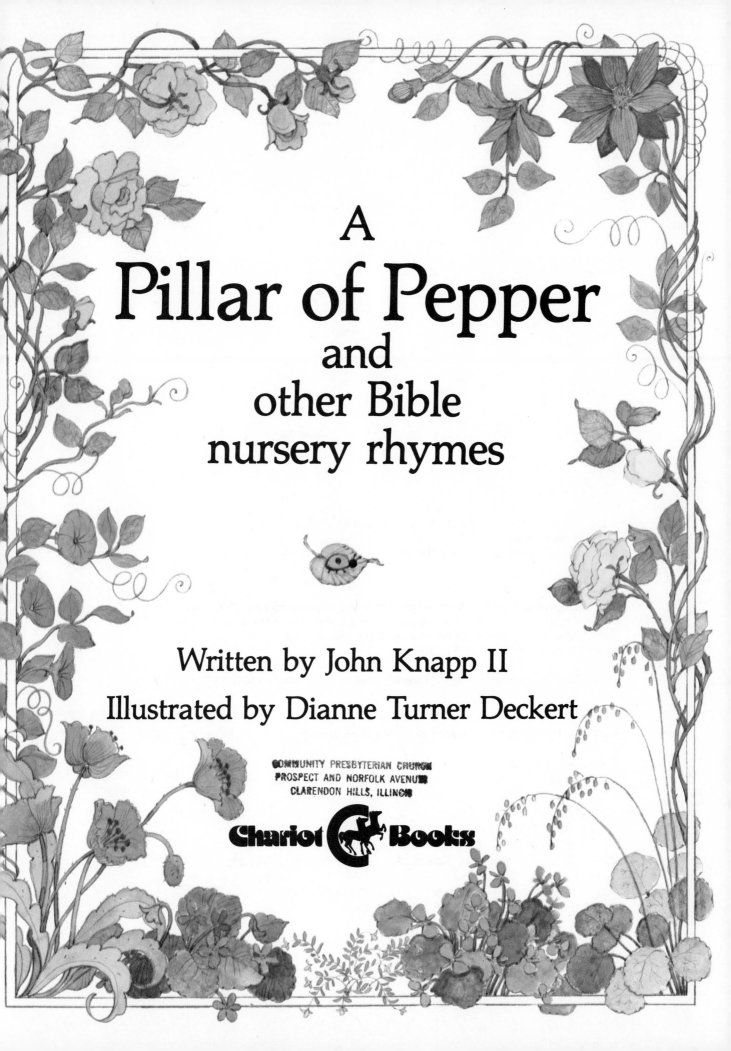

Written by John Knapp II

Illustrated by Dianne Turner Deckert

Chariot Books

A PILLAR OF PEPPER AND OTHER BIBLE NURSERY RHYMES
© 1982 John Knapp II
Illustrations © 1982 Dianne Turner Deckert

"Once David Was a Shepherd Boy" previously appeared in *Eternity* magazine.

Library of Congress Cataloging in Publication Data

Knapp, John, 1940-
    A pillar of pepper, and other Bible nursery rhymes.

    (Chariot books)
    Includes index.
    1. Bible--History of Biblical events--Poetry.
2. Children's poetry, American. I. Deckert, Dianne
Turner. II. Title.
PS3561.N33P5   811'.54   82-1489
ISBN 0-89191-559-1   AACR2

This book is dedicated to my wife Karen
and to my children Ethan, Phoebe, Eli, and Andrew

also to: Noah, Joshua, Megan, Kirstin, Courtney, Mandy, Scott,
David, Janelle, Mechele, Steven, Christine, Natalie, and Julie

and to Dave, Mark, Tom Paul, Eric, Sandra, and Leslie

and to the children of the Alliance Church of Oswego, New York
and the First Presbyterian Church of Montrose, Pennsylvania

Contents

ABOUT THE BIBLE

NEW TESTAMENT POEMS

A Regular Preface

(since most books have one)

The manuscript was nearly finished, and my second grader was once again hanging over my shoulder—literally hanging. Scraps of paper lay everywhere, suggesting my uncertainty.

"You know what I've done, son. But what should I say in the preface?"

"What's a preface?" Ethan asked.

I explained.

"You should say 'Read what you want,' and 'Stop when you want,' " he offered.

"Anything else?"

"Don't read it all at once. It would take a long time," he added.

I agree. But let me add a bit more. The rhymes are based upon the Bible references printed beneath them, and for the most part have been arranged sequentially—from Genesis to Revelation. We had to order them some way, and this way seemed to make the most sense. You will notice that some rhymes are short, others are long, some are easy, while others may seem difficult. But I think that's OK. The rhymes are for anyone who wants to try them—in any order. And now I must admit that I wrote them, and rewrote them, and rewrote them (and would rewrite them again if I had a chance) as I shared them with my wife and three children over our evening meals for more than a year. We hope you enjoy them as much as we have. My family and I offer them in this book in the name of Jesus Christ, who has given us much more than we deserve.

Another Preface

(for those who like small print)

Most of all, I hope you enjoy the rhymes in this book—enjoy them for their own sake. Many an evening my children and I have recited these, and their earlier versions, back and forth across the dinner table after we blew the candles out. And I think we were all better for it. If we learned something, it was in spite of ourselves. We really didn't work at it.

Enjoyment. What, specifically, do young children like in literature? That's difficult to answer. I think I know why my three-year-old son marches through our living room reciting "Joseph's Egyptian Jail Song"—it sounds good. But my five-year-old daughter's fascination with "The Bramble King," about an obscure fable from the Book of Judges, puzzles me. I'm not sure I completely understand what I wrote, or the biblical source I used.

Scholars have suggested that the first appeal of classic nursery literature is the way it sounds—the way the words tumble out when it is recited. We use words like "meter," "rhythm," "accent," and "rhyme" to describe such tumbling. In this book special attention has been paid to the sound of words. ("Rahab was a pretty girl/ Who liked to primp and strut./ Neighbors thought her very haughty—/ Naughty as can be! But/ . . .")

To those who share traditional nursery rhymes with children, as I do, it soon becomes obvious that the young enjoy much that they do not, and cannot, understand. For example, children happily accept the "tuffets," "pease porridge," and "curds and whey" of Mother Goose. Children welcome what "seems right." They are not yet yoked to the adult "duty" of explaining.

Because of their open-mindedness, I have let myself become adventurous with words in this book. And not a child I have encountered has batted an eye over such "complication." As a parent and former elementary school teacher, I have long been aware of the uncanny language ability of children in their early years—the poet Kornei Chukovsky calls it "linguistic genius." For a short time in nearly every preschooler's life, he learns as many as a dozen or more words a day—and this is, of course, from what he hears, not from dictionaries. The meanings of new words, if needed, emerge from their context. Rhymes and other nursery literature can be powerful language builders. And children *enjoy* gathering in new words when they are left to themselves to do it.

Some incidents of human drama that children enjoy may at first seem too perplexing, or too violent for young ears. Should children be shielded from pain, disease, and death in literature? Most teachers and scholars say no—not usually. Children already know these exist, more than we realize. In fact, children are often reassured by a brisk, but harsh, story in which justice is meted out, satisfying their sense of fair play (as in "Joseph's Coat" and "Ananias").

They respond to moments when genuine love intercedes and conquers evil, and mercy wipes away tragedy (as in "Jerusalem's Temple" and "Ten Poor Lepers"). They are more curious about, than disturbed by, events that offer no easy explanation (as in "King Solomon").

Nicholas Tucker, Bruno Bettleheim, and others have pointed out that much literature that first seems violent can actually have a positive effect upon children. In the Bible, as in classic fairy tales, children can see that good conquers evil. They are given hope, precious hope. "Bad things" which are talked about out loud—even if only through rhymes or stories—are less likely to be brooded over privately. Children *enjoy* overcoming their fears. They deserve the opportunity to see both sides of life in literature.

But enough of enjoyment. I am also concerned about what knowledge we Christians have. Often it is very little. As a Sunday School teacher I have become alarmed at how many children arrive at class, week after week, with God's Word tucked under their arms, but very little of it up in their heads. Too few children have a satisfactory overview of biblical history. Few know enough basic facts to fully appreciate God's plan for the ages. For example, many Christian teens who have attended church for years cannot trace the lineage of Abraham to his great-grandson Joseph (as in "Joseph's Egyptian Jail Song") or put Noah, Moses, David, and Jonah in chronological order (as in "Forty Days").

I hope that *A Pillar of Pepper* can help children learn about the Bible. Possessing facts, of course, does not make anyone a Christian. But with information a child can be led to Christ, and a child who already believes can become more firmly established.

I am indebted to many for this book. All the children who heard me out were patient beyond their years. Some of my captive university students gave helpful feedback. I especially want to thank my English colleagues at State University of New York: Dr. Judith Moore and Dr. Inez Alfors for their detailed reactions to most of the rhymes, and for their suggestions and support for this project; and Professor Lewis Turco for alerting me to the possibilities and problems of writing in traditional forms. I am grateful to Susan Zitzman of David C. Cook Publishing for her careful editing.

Most of all, I want to thank my wife Karen who was patient and encouraging when I needed her, especially in getting started and getting finished.

And I must thank my seven-year-old son Ethan who, very obligingly, learned to read during the course of preparing this manuscript. Without him hanging over my shoulder and challenging why I thought my inked-in revisions were better than what I crossed out, this book would be less than it is—and would have been much less fun to put together.

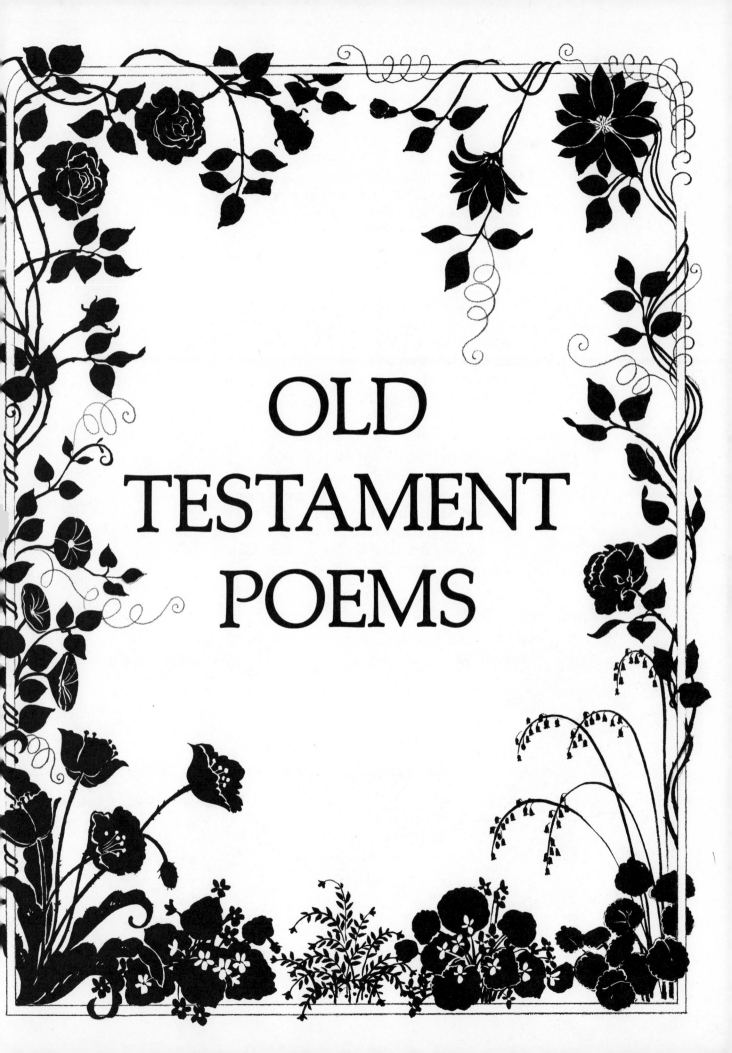

OLD
TESTAMENT
POEMS

The Creation

Sunday was first, the very first day
That matter unfolded in space,
And that great clock, time, began its long count,
As God put every atom in place.
   And before the beginning was done,
     God's Spirit moved over Day 1, Day 1,
     God's Spirit moved over Day 1.

On Monday God made enormous clouds
Out of water flung high in the air;
They rose from the sea on the earth below
Before the dry land was there.
   The earth was all wet when God was through
     Shaping the sky on Day 2, Day 2,
     Shaping the sky on Day 2.

On Tuesday God moved the seas aside
So soil and rock could appear.
The earth opened up to the first green plants,
And food of all kinds was here.
   Light came through thick clouds to shower each tree
     That sprang from the earth on Day 3, Day 3,
     That sprang from the earth on Day 3.

On Wednesday the watery clouds broke apart
That surrounded the earth on high;
The planets and sun, the moon and the stars
Were unmasked in the clearing sky.
   The heavens at last cracked open their door
   To the sun streaking over Day 4, Day 4,
   To the sun streaking over Day 4.

On Thursday animals burst on the scene—
Fishes, reptiles, and birds;
Brontosaurus came forth, pterodactyl flew
When the word of the Master was heard.
   Some kinds of animals still alive
   Took their first steps on Day 5, Day 5,
   Took their first steps on Day 5.

On Friday came elephants, cattle, and apes,
Every mammal according to plan.
The earth—almost done—only lacked one thing,
So God out of dust made man.
   Heavenly image gave shape to that mix
   When God crowned his work on Day 6, Day 6,
   When God crowned his work on Day 6.

On the Sabbath God rested from all that he did
Making animals, plants, and sea;
   All special building had ended, he knew,
   Except for creating in me, in me,
   Creating in me—and you.

Genesis 1:1—2:3

The Garden of Eden

Why was the greatest garden plot
The one that grew in Eden?
'Cause grapes and peas and lima beans there
Never needed weedin'.

Genesis 2:8—3:19

Eden Was Perfect

Eden was perfect
Till Eve burst the bubble;
She ate what she shouldn't . . .
Then came the trouble.

Genesis 2:8—3:24

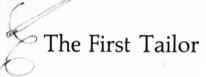

The First Tailor

The very first tailor
Was Eve's husband, Adam,
Who needed some pants
Before anyone had 'em.

He sinned before
Harvesting cotton or flax,
So he stitched up some fig leaves
To make the first slacks.

Genesis 3:1-7

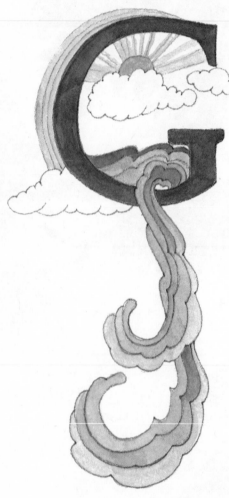

Noah

God told old Noah
To make him a boat,
So when everything else sank,
Something would float.

Genesis 6–8

Abraham and Sarah

Abraham laughed!
It wasn't a bother
At the age of one hundred
To be a new father.

Even Sarah at ninety
With Baby Isaác
Never once ever thought
About giving him back.

Genesis 17:15-19; 21:1-3

Esau

Isaac's son Esau
Caused one big to-do
When he swapped his birthright
For a pot full of stew.

Genesis 25:24-34

A Pillar of Pepper

Since Mrs. Lot sinned
And was clearly at fault,
God let her change into
A pillar of salt.

But when Miriam sinned
She became a poor leper
Instead of some thing like
A pillar of pepper.

Since sinning may change us
In ways you can see,
I plan to be good
So you'll recognize me.

But recognize also,
I plan to obey
Because Jesus, my Savior,
Wants it that way.

Genesis 19:15-26
Numbers 12

Joseph's Coat

J oseph's coat had too many colors,
Or so murmured ten of his jealous brothers
Who sold him to Egypt to work as a slave,
And back to their father his coat gave.

Though minus his coat in Egypt land,
Joseph was protected by God's right hand;
Though thrown in jail for something sinister,
Pharaoh made Joseph the next Prime Minister.

Genesis 37; 39:1—41:44

Joseph's Egyptian Jail Song

(A Marching Rhyme)

Great-grandfather .... *Abraham*
Marched into the .. Promised Land

Grandfather .... *Isaac*
Did not .... turn back

Uncle .... *Esau*
Hot soup .... he saw

My father .... *Jacob*
Twelve sons .... raised up

My mother .... *Rachel*
Loved me .... real well

I am .... *Joseph*
One who .... knows if

God is .... with me
I can .... not fail

Even though .... Potiphar
Put me .... in jail

Genesis 39

Moses' Rod

oses, O Moses,
Servant of God,
Where do you keep
That unusual rod?

We saw you once
A wooden stick take;
You flung it down
And it hissed as a snake.

Then down dipped your hand,
This snake up to pick,
And that ugly reptile
Changed back to a stick.

Exodus 4:1-5

The Food from God

Asked a grumbling child named Hannah,
"Could I have an orange or banana?
I've just had enough
Of this fluffy white stuff;
It's boring to only eat manna!"

Then to Hannah her mom did declare,
"Perceive how our cupboard is bare!
While the desert we wander,
Of this food get fonder,
'Cause manna tastes better than air!"

Exodus 16
Numbers 11:4-10

Rahab

Rahab was a pretty girl
Who liked to primp and strut.
Neighbors thought her very haughty—
Naughty as can be! But

Secretly she heard God's voice
And acted on the matter.
In Jericho she saved two spies
With her red rope ladder.

Joshua 2:1-24; 6:17-25

Deborah and Barak

The prophetess Deborah
Was Israel's fourth judge;
From the way of Jehovah
She never would budge.

Her general named Barak
Led soldiers with pride,
But only when Deborah
Marched right by his side.

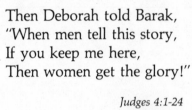

Then Deborah told Barak,
"When men tell this story,
If you keep me here,
Then women get the glory!"

Judges 4:1-24

General Gideon

General Gideon
With so many men,
Told those who were scared
To march home again.

Gideon battled
With only the best,
Trusting the Lord
To handle the rest.

Judges 7:1-25

The Bramble King

Here's a strange forest story
That has an odd ring:
It seems that the trees
Began wanting a king.
They had branches and leaves,
But no lips 'nor head,
Yet the trees could speak clearly,
And here's what they said:

"Olive Tree, Olive Tree,
Come be our king!"

But the Olive refused
To be pestered and used,
Saying, "I'm too fat
To think about that!"
And that was the end of the thing, the thing;
That was the end of the thing.

So they asked the Fig
Standing almost as big:
"Fig Tree, O Fig Tree,
Come be our king!"

But the Fig Tree refused
To be pestered and used,
Saying, "I'm too sweet
Making good fruit to eat!"
And that was the end of the thing, the thing;
That was the end of the thing.

So they asked the Grape,
In spite of his shape:
"Grape Vine, O Grape Vine,
Come be our king!"

But the Grape Vine refused
To be pestered and used,
Saying, "All of my time
I must spend making wine!"
And that was the end of the thing, the thing;
That was the end of the thing.

So they took a big gamble
And asked an old Bramble:
"Bramble, O Bramble,
Come be our king!"

When the Bramble said, "Yes!"
He caused such a mess,
That that was the end of the thing, the thing;
The final last end of the thing.

Judges 9:7-20

Samuel and Eli

When late at night he heard his name,
Little Samuel said,
"Here am I, here am I,"
And hopped out of bed.

"But I didn't call you!"
Mumbled old Eli.
"Run back to your own room
And shut your eyes!"

When he heard his name again,
Little Samuel said,
"Here am I, here am I,"
And hopped out of bed.

"But I didn't call you!"
Again said the priest,
So he sent the boy away
And conversation ceased.

When he heard his name again,
Little Samuel said,
"Here am I, here am I,"
And hopped out of bed.

Eli recognized at last
This shouldn't be ignored,
So he said to Samuel,
"This voice must be the Lord!"

When Samuel heard his name again,
He answered loud and clear,
"I'm just a boy, O Lord, my God,
But still I want to hear!"

So on one special night that followed
Just a usual day,
God found one young and willing
To hear what he would say.

1 Samuel 3:1-18

The Tabernacle

Long before Jesus
Came down to the earth,
Before the first Christmas,
The time of his birth,

God came to Israel,
From heaven he went,
To meet with mankind
In a colorful tent.

Surrounded by a curtain,
This tent had a place
Reserved for a priest
To meet God face-to-face.

And once a year only
The High Priest went in,
Crawling under the curtain
To confess Israel's sin.

Exodus 26:30-35
Leviticus 16

The Stolen Ark

Terrible Dagon
And God's Holy Ark
Stood side by side
In Ashdod in the dark.

The very next day
When light crept through the door,
Terrible Dagon
Lay sprawled on the floor.

Then the Philistines
Had their strongest men
Prop up old Dagon
By God's Ark again.

Terrible Dagon
And God's Holy Ark
Once again stood
In Ashdod in the dark.

The very next day
To everyone's dread,
Dagon lay broken
And minus his head.

Then the Philistines
Began to get sick:
They itched and they swelled up;
Their legs got so thick

That they cried, "The Lord's Ark
Is behind this bad news!"
So that's why they carried it
Back to the Jews.

1 Samuel 5:1—7:1

Jesse's Small Son

The Lord said to Samuel,
"You are to go choose
From the eight sons of Jesse
A king for the Jews."

Eliab marched in,
Who was the first son;
He was handsome and tall,
But he wasn't the one.

Abinadab entered,
A manly young Jew,
But the Lord said to Samuel,
"Don't pick Number Two."

Then Jesse called Shammah,
As straight as a tree;
But again the Lord said,
"It's not Number Three."

Then one by one,
Four more sons walked in,
And the Lord said to Samuel,
"No," four times again.

"Are these all?" Samuel asked.
"Now let's get this straight—
These sons number seven;
I thought you had eight!"

Jesse was puzzled,
His wonder ran deep.
"But my last son's a small boy
Out tending the sheep!"

Then Samuel told Jesse,
"I won't sit for lunch
Until I've seen *this* son,
So bring him at once!"

When David walked in,
Samuel said, "That's the one!
I anoint you the king;
God wants this last son."

Beauty and strength
Don't make leaders of men;
While we see just the outside,
God sees what's within.

1 Samuel 16:1-13

Five Stones

tone Number One David put in his bag;
For all that we know, for all that we care,
Stone Number One is still there.

Stone Number Two David put in his bag;
For all that we know, for all that we care,
Stone Number Two is still there.

Stone Number Three David put in his bag;
For all that we know, for all that we care,
Stone Number Three is still there.

Stone Number Four David put in his bag;
For all that we know, for all that we care,
Stone Number Four is still there.

Stone Number Five David put in his bag;
But from all that we know, (and we certainly care!)
Stone Number Five is not there!

Smooth and well-rounded, and ready to fling,
This is the stone David picked for his sling.
This is the stone that God let him use
To stop old Goliath and save all the Jews.

1 Samuel 17:1-58

David, the General

David, the general,
Had little to fear;
He prayed before fighting
With arrows and spear.

David, the general,
Swung a sharp sword;
But in battle above all
He trusted the Lord.

Psalms 44:6-8

Once David Was a Shepherd Boy

Once David was a shepherd boy
With many ewes and rams,
Who had to kill a lion
To save the little lambs.

Once David was a soldier boy
Who could not use a spear,
So he slew a giant with a sling
(With faith he conquered fear).

Later David reigned as king
Of ancient Israel,
Yet each day he'd always pray
So God would rule as well.

King David was a grandpa too,
And do not think this odd: .
To his children's children's children
Was born the Son of God.

1 Samuel 17:34-50
Psalms 86:3
Matthew 1:1-17

Absalom

Absalom, Absalom
Israel's prince,
After three thousand years
We remember you since

Your mule ran a dirt road
Unfortunately where,
Tree branches bent too low
And tangled your hair.

Absalom's, Absalom's
Royal head hung
Ruling just wind
That blew where he swung.

2 Samuel 18:9-10

Ethan, the Ezrahite

Early to bed
Makes a bright early riser,
Ethan was smart,
But King Solomon wiser.

1 Kings 4:29-31
Author of Psalm 89

The Land of Milk and Honey

Hundreds of bees
Make sweet honey in hives;
In Solomon's palace
Live one thousand wives.

Hundreds of cows
Make milk in the stable;
Can you count all the seats
Around Solomon's table?

When King Solomon reigned
In Israel land,
There was plenty of milk
And sweet honey on hand.

Joshua 5:6
1 Kings 11:3

King Solomon

Solomon, Solomon,
Wonderfully wise,
How could you get married
To one thousand wives?

If God gave you wisdom,
Then how could you falter,
With wife after wife
Building idol and altar?

Your life in old age
Fills me with distress;
Why did you slowly
Love God less and less?

If you were so wise,
I hardly can see
How things will go better
With simpleton me!

Deuteronomy 17:14-17
1 Kings 11:1-13

King Jereboam

When Jereboam had God's Word,
When King Jerry finally heard
That God would bless him, it's absurd
To think he would become a nerd!
But that is simply what occurred.

1 Kings 11:28-38; 14:7-10

Elijah and the Prophets of Baal

Testing the Lord,
Testing the Lord,
God's chosen people
Begin to turn toward

The prophets of Baal,
The prophets of Baal,
Prophets of evil
Who only can fail.

Cooler than ice,
Cooler than ice,
The prophets of Baal
Put a sacrifice

On an altar of stone,
An altar of stone,
To prove to the people
Baal is God alone.

Jumping and prancing,
Jumping and prancing,
Hundreds of prophets
Are shouting and dancing

From sunrise at seven
To way past eleven,
Begging old Baal
To send fire from heaven.

Look at them leap
As they wail and they weep
Elijah then laughs,
"Could Baal be asleep?

"Can't you inspire
Your god to send fire?
For if Baal refuses,
He looks like a liar!"

But there isn't a spark,
Not even a spark
As the prophets of Baal
Dance into the dark.

"Give Elijah a turn!
Give Elijah a turn!"
The grumbling people
Want something to burn.

So Elijah alone,
Elijah alone,
Builds quickly an altar
Stone upon stone.

And next comes the wood,
Kindling wood
To lie under the sacrifice
Just where it should.

Now jugs of water,
"Bring jugs of water;
Soak," says Elijah,
"God's holy altar!"

With never a doubt,
Not one single doubt,
Elijah now cries
To the Lord with a shout,

"Lord, if you choose,
Proclaim now the news
That *only Jehovah
Is God of the Jews!*"

Then to the wonder,
Amazement of all,
Down from the heavens
Fire does fall:
Licking up sacrifice—
Both meat and bones;
Burning up wood;
And even the stones;
Boiling water
Into scalding steam,
Till the altar now *isn't*—
Just like a dream!

When Israel saw
Such almighty power
Their faith in old Baal
Went suddenly sour.
They begged God's forgiveness
When everything burned,
And back to Jehovah
His people returned.

1 Kings 18:17-40

55

Sick Captain Naaman

(A One-act Play)

Characters: Captain Naaman, Naaman's faithful servant, Narrator
Setting: The bank of the Jordan River. Naaman and his servant are talking to each other.

Servant: Naaman, dear master,
All covered with spots,
What are you thinking,
What are your thoughts?

Naaman: **Elisha, the prophet,
Said God would deliver,
If seven times under
I dip in this river.**

Narrator: *So handily, spandily,
Naaman walked in;
He waded in water
Up to his chin.*

Servant: Naaman, dear master,
All covered with spots,
Now what are you thinking,
What are your thoughts?

Naaman: **This Jordan is muddy
And nasty. Oh, please!
I'd rather stay sick,
And keep my disease!**

Narrator: *Still handily, spandily,
Naaman stayed in;
He stood in the water
Up to his chin.*

Servant: Naaman, dear master,
All covered with spots,
Now what are you thinking,
What are your thoughts?

Naaman: **I'm beginning to shiver,**
This water's so cool;
My clothes are all clammy,
I feel like a fool!

Servant: Yet seven times under,
Elisha had said;
You must pinch your nose shut,
And push down your head!

Naaman: **But this Jordan is muddy**
And nasty. Oh, please!
I'd rather stay sick,
And keep my disease!

Narrator: Still handily, spandily,
Naaman stayed in;
He stood in the water
Up to his chin.

Then seven whole times,
Naaman ducked under,
Rising at last,
Eyes open in wonder.

His leprosy left
Without leaving a trace;
There didn't remain
A white spot on his face!

Servant: Naaman, dear master,
Now where are your spots?
What are you thinking,
What are your thoughts?

2 Kings 5: 1-14

57

Two and Forty Evil Men

Once two and forty evil men
The devil did corrupt.
They called Elisha "Old Bald Head,"
And then bears beat them up.

2 Kings 2:23-24

The Lost Axhead

Elisha's woodcutter
Stopped dead in his tracks,
When off from the handle
Flew the head of his ax.

Looking up, the poor cutter
Watched, with a shiver,
The axhead he'd borrowed
Splash into the river.

Elisha then threw
A stick toward that same spot,
And that lifeless old axhead
Swam up to the top.

2 Kings 6:1-7

The Boy King

Crown the prince, Josiah!
Make him Chief of State.
Josiah wants to serve the Lord
Although he's only eight!

2 Kings 22:1-2

King Nebuchadnezzar

King Nebuchadnezzar
Thought he was a treasure
(Though really he was a big clod).
He said, "Pray to me,
For can you not see
That I'm much more special than God?"

Soon this foolish king
Messed up everything.
(His head must have been filled with rocks.)
Then for seven long years,
In sorrow and tears,
God made him eat grass like an ox.

Daniel 3, 4

Daniel

Some proud Persian princes
Persisted in tryin'
To get Prophet Daniel
Inside of a lion.

But God only let them
Get Dan in the den,
Where he closed every jaw,
Until the time when

The king saw God's power,
The princes as sinners,
And so *they* became
The next lion den dinners.

Daniel 6

The Prophet Hosea

The prophet, Hosea,
Stirred up quite a row
When he preached that God's people
Behaved like a cow!

As stupid as that?
Whom do you kid?
How could such good folk
Become so backslid?

But God's chosen people
Were clearly to blame,
For down before idols
They'd wallowed in shame.

Still God in his love
Let Hosea be sent
To wake up his people
So they would repent.

Hosea 4:15-19; 14:1-9

The Prophet Micah

Long ago, I have a hunch,
Micah's whole report
You could hear while eating lunch;
His message was that short.

Nonetheless his prophecy
Contained this precious gem:
Christ would come eventually
From tiny Bethlehem.

Micah 5:2

Jonah

I n the town of Nineveh
The children misbehaved,
And all their mothers ranted,
While all their fathers raved.

So to the town of Nineveh
God called a missionary,
But Jonah sailed the other way
For preaching there was scary.

But when a wild storm arose
From which they could not flee,
The sailors blamed poor Jonah,
And flung him in the sea.

Thinking he could run from God
Proved a foolish wish,
For God caught up with Jonah
In the stomach of a fish.

Now a prophet who was sorry
Wasn't food the fish had craved,
So he threw up Jonah on the shore
And Nineveh was saved.

Book of Jonah

Forty Days

Twenty, thirty, forty days . . .
It rained, and rained, and rained;
Yet Noah's boat rode out the Flood
When nothing else remained.

Twenty, thirty, forty days . . .
Moses climbed up high;
And on the mountain God wrote down,
"Do not steal or lie."

Twenty, thirty, forty days . . .
Terror stalked the land,
Until Goliath lost his head
When David took command.

Twenty, thirty, forty days
Were left until the end;
So Jonah preached to Nineveh
Of judgment God would send.

Twenty, thirty, forty . . .
Forty days of hunger—
Satan tempted Jesus then;
Is it any wonder?

Twenty, thirty, forty-one . . .
We'll only do this once;
Since forty-one means nothing,
We'll stop and have our lunch.

Genesis 6:1—8:22
Exodus 19:1—20:17; 34:1-4, 28
1 Samuel 17:1-54
Book of Jonah
Matthew 4:1-11

ABOUT THE BIBLE

Reading My Bible

Fee, Fie, Foe, Fiddle,
My Bible opens flat to the middle;
Now under my palms
Are some words from the Psalms
Which I read without any more diddle.

God's Word

 A admired it.

B believed it.

 C carried it.

 D defended it.

 E enjoyed it.

 F feasted upon it.

 G gleaned it.

H held it.

 I interpreted it.

 J judged it.

K kept it.

L loved it.

 M memorized it.

 N needed it.

 O opened it.

P preached it.

 Q quoted it.

 R read it.

 S studied it.

 T taught it.

 U understood it.

V valued it.

 **W** wondered about it.

 X examined it.

 Y yielded to it.

 Z zealously hid it in his heart.

Five Sunday Night Dreams
Dream 1: Books of the Law

Genesis, Exodus, Leviticus, Numbers,
Sat on a picket fence, eating cucumbers.
"What a funny sight to see!"
Said happy *Deuteronomy.*

Dream 2: Books of History

It simply isn't quite the truth
That *Joshua* really *Judges Ruth,*
That *Samuel One* the right to rule,
Or *Samuel Two* went back to school.
For they rejected royal things
Owned by the *First* and *Second Kings.*
And if *One Chronicles* all they did,
And writes these *Chronicles Two,*
Then *Ezra* and
Nehemiah can
Show *Esther* that we're through.

Dream 3: Books of Poetry

Job in his robe
Without any qualms,
Stepped to the podium
And read some *Psalms*.
When he stumbled over
Six enormous words,
He flipped the dusty pages
Till he found *Proverbs*.
But he finished with a sneeze, plus
He tripped on his thongs;
"Ec—ec—*Ecclesiastes*!" was
His final *Song of Songs*.

Dream 4: Major Prophets

To *Isaiah, Jeremiah*
Cried, "Oh, *Lamentations!*
Ezekiel and *Daniel* ate up
All our dinner rations!"

Dream 5:Minor Prophets

Hosea and *Joel*
Climbed up a flag pole
Two meters above even *Amos;*
Up came *Obadiah*
Who went even high-ah
Than *Jonah* (who was much more famous).
Then *Micah* and *Nahum,*
Up also they cay-um.
Yet high on that pole,
They were low on their luck;
Although above others,
These seven were stuck.

Now call for five good men
With ladder and truck;
Call for the resources
Of Chief *Habakkúk.*
With him in his engine
Comes kind *Zephaniah;*
He thinks, as the others,
That there is a fie-ah.
"*Haggai,* drop that hose!"
Then shrieks *Zechariah,*
"*Malachi,* it's your net
These poor men require!"

Three Monday Morning Daydreams
Daydream 1

Matthew, Mark, Luke, and *John*
Took their trusty *Acts*
And tried to chop a maple down
To pay the *Romans* tax.
This all led to a battle,
Which the good *Corinthians One,*
But *Two Corinthians* wondered how,
While they were on the run.

AEIO T

Daydream 2

A, E, I, O,
But chuck away the *U.*
The first four vowels are useful;
Now I'll show why this is true:
There's *A*'s in those *Galatians;*
E starts *Ephesians* right;
I fills up *Philippians*
Which puts the end in sight;
The *O*'s found in *Colossians*
Number only two.
Now closely look at letter *T*
Since off I threw the *U:*
If you please, there are five *T*'s
That are arranged just so:
Thessalonians One and *Two*
Start an alphabetic row;
First and *Second Timothy*
Next line up beside us;
Now I can end my second dream,
If I only mention *Titus.*

Daydream 3

Philemon counted *Hebrews;*
What more letters will there be?
James has one and *Peter* two
While *John* has even three.
Now don't be rude to tiny *Jude,*
Who without hesitation,
Dreams a dream that now must end
Just like this *Revelation.*

How Many Books?

Take the letters in "Old"
And count them for me;
If you do this
You will get only 3.
Now look at "Testament"
And you will find
That the letters in this word
Will always be 9.

If you put these numbers
Side by side on a line,
The result of such writing
Becomes 39.
And 39 books are all that were meant
To make up what we call the Old Testament.

Take the letters in "New"
And count them for me;
And just like before,
You only get 3.
Now look at "Testament"
And you will find
That the letters in this word
Again will be 9.

If you take these numbers
And then multiply,
The 27 you get
Is not quite so high.
But 27 books are all that were meant
To make up what we call the New Testament.

$$3 \times 9 = 27$$

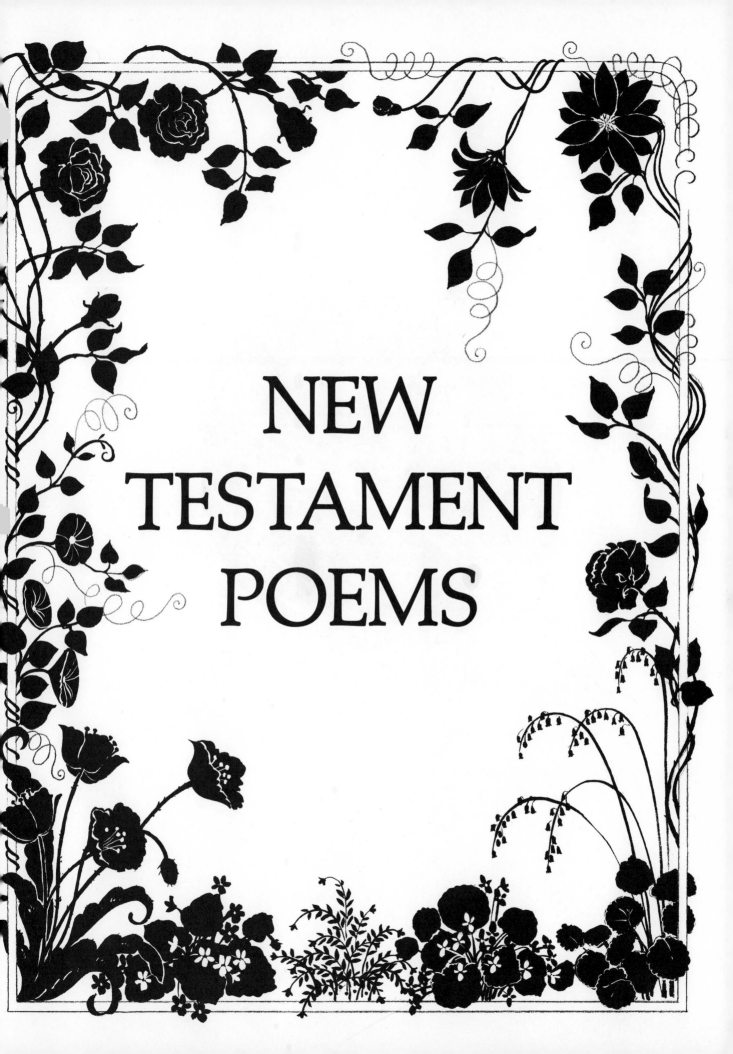

NEW TESTAMENT POEMS

Before Anything Was

Before anything was,
    there was the Word,
But what was the Word
    I do wonder?

The Word was none other
    than Jesus Christ
Who lives with his Father
    up yonder.

John 1:1

The First Christmas Eve
(Before anyone knew about Christmas)

I wish that I could move to Rome;
Nothing happens here at home.
I hop in bed, "Dear Lord . . . Amen,"
And snuggle down in Bethlehem.
If I could travel wide and far,
I'd see *much more* than one bright star!

(Moral: People bored and brooding
May miss what the Lord is doing.)

Matthew 2:1-2

Christmas Morn

What would the people
    of Bethlehem say,
If they only knew
    that two blocks away
The awaited Messiah
    had come to their town
With a halo of hay
    instead of a crown?

Luke 2

The Manger

Once in a feeding trough
My Savior lay,
His very first mattress
A handful of hay.

Luke 2:7

John the Baptist

When John the Baptist
Preached of sin,
The people realized
They had to change
Their nasty ways,
And also be baptized.

Luke 3:1-18

The Sermon on the Mount

Jesus said so many things
While preaching on the mount,
That when I tried to catch them all,
My fingers lost the count.

Matthew 5-7

Be Wise

Be wise as a snake
Yet sweet as a dove;
Think as hard as you can
Just as long as you love.

Matthew 10:16
1 Corinthians 13:1

Five Loaves

nly five loaves of bread
And two very small fishes,
When blessed by Christ Jesus,
Filled five thousand dishes.

John 6:1-13

A Pharisee

I hope that I shall never be
As foolish as a Pharisee

Who thinks that it's so very cool,
Memorizing every rule.

At worship he can hardly wait
To plink his coins into the plate.

A Pharisee stands tall to pray
So no one misses what he'll say.

And if you ask him out to eat,
He grabs himself the finest seat.

A Pharisee is often loud,
Rarely shy, but proud, real proud

Of what he knows and what he does,
Of what he is, of what he was.

A Pharisee so narrow-minded
Fools himself; his eyes are blinded

To the Lord who, way back then,
Said, "First, you must be born again."

Luke 11:37-44
John 3:1-21

92

A Sadduccee

Inside of every Sadduccee
There lurks a giant frown:
He thinks when he is buried,
He'll stay
        down

            in the ground.

Luke 20:27
Acts 23:8

93

From a Fish's Mouth

Best, better, good,
Going downhill to worsen,
Poor Apostle Peter
Met the Roman tax person.

Then Jesus said to Peter,
"Do not think it funny
When you open up a fish's mouth
To find some tax money!"

Matthew 17:24-27

Ten Poor Lepers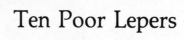

Ten poor lepers,
  sick as they could be,
Lived by themselves
  in the land of Galilee.

Then the Son of Man
  came walking down the road.
"Oh, heal us!" they cried,
  "We bear a heavy load!"

The Lord Jesus Christ
  was touched in his soul;
He spoke unto the ten men
  and all were made whole.

- Leper Number 1 left to find his brother,
- Leper Number 2 ran home to his mother,
- Leper Number 3 set out to get a wife,
- Leper Number 4 simply ran for his life.
- Leper Number 5 paused to count his money,
- Leper Number 6 bought some jam and honey,
- Leper Number 7 wondered what to do,
- Leper Number 8 was glad he was a Jew,
- Leper Number 9 said, "What else is new?"

But Leper Number 10,
  on his knees he fell,
Crying, "Thank you, Lord Jesus,
  for making me well!"

This poor leper
  had his body made new,
But when he thanked Jesus,
  his heart was healed, too.

Luke 17:11-19

Conversations at Martha's and Mary's

artha, Martha,
Sweep the hearth, a
Mountain of ashes lie there.
And when you are done,
Come back on the run,
Because Mary is being unfair."

"Mary, Mary,
Why are you very
Unkind to your sister so true?
You simply can't leave us
For all day with Jesus;
We've guests! There is work we must do!"

"Jesus, Jesus,
Can you not see us?
Make Mary do her fair part!"
But Jesus said, "No,
For tomorrow I go,
And Mary's preparing her heart."

Luke 10:38-42

The Body of Lazarus

The body of Lazarus
Could be ignored;
Four days in the grave
Made it stiff as a board.

But when Jesus spoke to it,
Lazarus arose,
Awaking in praise
From his lips to his toes!

John 11:1-45; 12:9-11

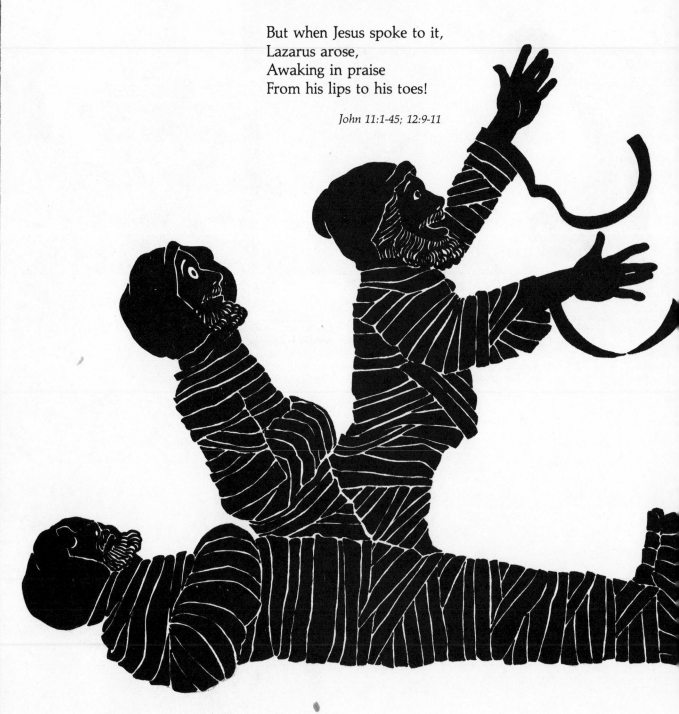

Zaccheus

Zaccheus was as short
As this odd poem about him;
He first saw the Lord
From a sycamore tree limb.

But if you consider
High places too scary,
You can meet Jesus
Somewhere ordinary.

Luke 19:1-9

Mary and Judas

Mary of Bethany,
We presume,
Loved more than gold
Her expensive perfume.

Then why is she pouring it
All over Jesus?
Is Mary mixed up,
Or trying to tease us?

Judas Iscariot,
We presume,
Got very enraged
As he watched in the room.

"For the poor you could sell this,
And yet you refused;
You've wasted this perfume!"
His heart was confused.

Then Jesus said, "Judas,
Stop being so worried;
She's anointing my body
That soon must be buried."

John 12:1-8
Mark 14:3-9

Peter's Denial

Peter, Peter, look at Jesus!
Soldiers have snatched him away!
They're going to hurt him,
They're going to hurt him;
Don't you have something to say?

"Never, never did I know him!"
Peter was scared as he lied.
Then the cock crowed,
Then the cock crowed;
And Peter ran home and cried.

Mark 14:66-72

Pontius Pilate

See Pontius Pilate
Guiltily hasten,
To wash his pale hands
In a silvery basin.

Pontius Pilate
Knew all along,
That punishing Jesus
Was terribly wrong.

Matthew 27:11-24

Barabbas

arabbas the robber
Was terribly shocked,
When Pilate the judge
Had his jail door unlocked.

Barabbas the robber
Just could not see
Why Pilate the judge
Released him scot-free.

Matthew 27:15-26

The Born-again Thief

The born-again thief
Never once bent his knee
To thank the Lord Jesus
For setting him free.

Yet he praised his new master
Who hung by him there,
As both died on crosses
Stuck high in the air.

Luke 23:39-43

108

The Grave's a Place

The grave's a place to put you down,
So the story goes.
But Jesus told it differently,
And up from his he rose!

Mark 16:6

Easter Morning

In Jesus' tomb
There is plenty of room;
Don't take it from me;
Come in and see!

Sunshine pours in
Through a wide-open door,
But no one is here,
Just some stuff on the floor.

Careful! Don't trip on
Grave wrappings and shroud;
Step boldly over,
His friends are allowed.

You don't have to whisper
To honor the dead,
For Jesus has risen,
Just as he said!

Matthew 28:1-6
Luke 24:1-12
John 20:1-10

Cautious Thomas

Said cautious Thomas
Filled with doubt,
"Unless Christ Jesus
Comes about

And I can touch
His hands and feet,
My faith will never
Be complete!"

But all the doubt
Expressed that day
Later Jesus
Wiped away.

John 20:24-31

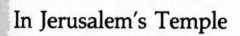

In Jerusalem's Temple

In Jerusalem's Temple
With God's Holy Word,
The apostles preached Jesus
And multitudes heard.

But when they declared
That Jesus had risen,
An angry high priest
Shut them all up in prison.

Then God sent an angel
With heavenly clout,
To open the jail doors
And shut them back *out!*

In Jerusalem's Temple
With God's Holy Word,
The apostles preached Jesus
And multitudes heard.

Acts 5:12-42

Ananias

There once was a man Ananias,
Who hid a most dishonest bias;
His gift to Saint Peter
Proved him such a cheater,
He fell down stone-dead on the dais.

Acts 5:1-11

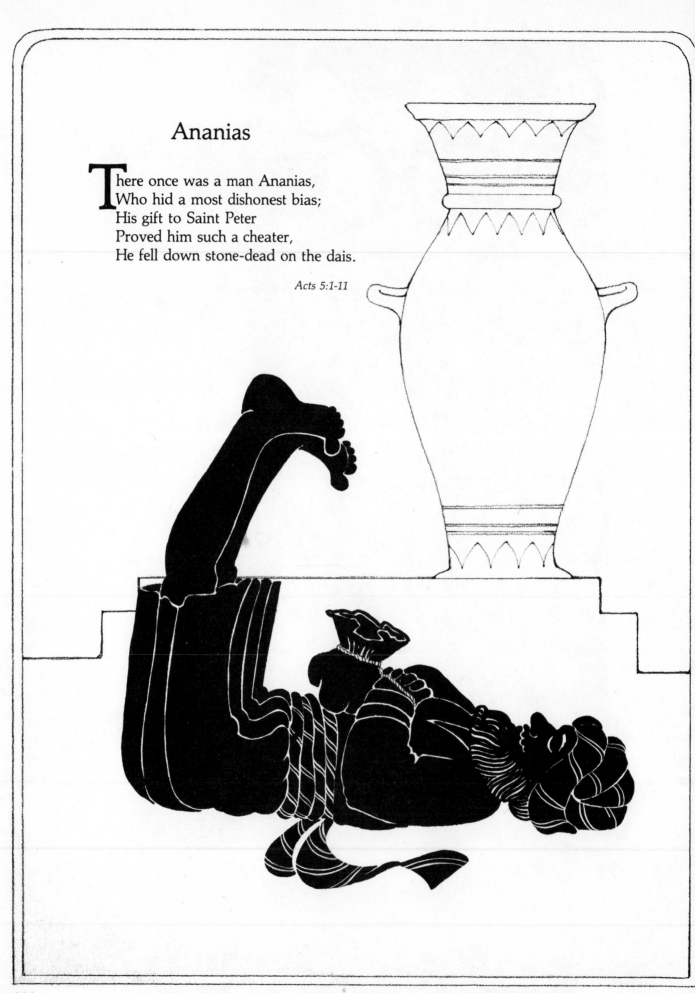

Once Paul Was a Bully

Once Paul was a bully, a serious pest,
Who bothered new Christians and gave them no rest.
But when he met Jesus,
(And doesn't that please us!)
The Christians by Paul were eventually blessed.

Acts 8:1-4; 9:1-20

Aquila and Priscilla

There once lived a man called Aquila
In a modest Corinthian villa;
Aquila made tents
For dollars and cents
With the help of his good wife Priscilla.

Acts 18:1-3

Poor, Sleepy Eutychus

Poor, sleepy Eutychus,
A-sittin' without squirmin',
Perching on a window ledge
To hear an endless sermon.

Now his eyes are droopy,
Sittin' way up high;
Poor, sleepy Eutychus
Is just about to die.

Saint Paul keeps on a-preachin'
To our hero snoozin' hard;
Then Euty leans into the air
And crashes in the yard.

But Paul is an apostle,
Quite unlike other men;
Down he runs to Eutychus
And gives him life again.

So if you're gonna sleep in church,
Don't from a window fall;
The man up front a-preachin'
Is not apostle Paul.

Acts 20:9-12

Forty Foolish Men

Forty very foolish men
Once took a foolish vow:
They swore they'd never eat again
Until they killed Saint Paul.

But Paul's nephew overheard
The foolish thing these men had said,
So soldiers ran to rescue Paul,
And the foolish forty starved instead. . . .

But did they really die this way?
Well, the Bible doesn't say.
So if you think they ate and drank,
You are a "doubting Thomas"!
Yet you're probably right, 'cause foolish men
Rarely keep a promise.

Acts 23:12-31

Phoebe, God's Helper

Phoebe, God's helper,
Once left her fine home,
To carry Paul's letter
To Christians in Rome.

Romans 16:1, 2

Demas

Demas, with Apostle Paul,
Served the Lord like Luke,
But the love he showed to all,
Proved later just a fluke.
Finally, Demas, one sad day,
Turned from God and ran away.

Colossians 4:14
2 Timothy 4:10

Aristarchus

If you aren't too fancy,
Just an ordinary carcass,
Consider the example
Of a man called Aristarchus.

Five times the Bible tells us
How his faith refused to bend;
Quietly he served the Lord,
Enduring to the end.

Acts 19:29
Acts 20:4
Acts 27:2
Colossians 4:10
Philemon 24

I'm Counting

Two, four, six, eight,
Seven come eleven;
I'm counting on my Savior
To take me up to heaven.

Romans 8:35-39

Two Sad Churches

Oh me ah, Oh my ah,
Oh me ah, Oh my ah,
Come see the church in old Thyatira.
People who went there were not very good;
Yet people who went there were not very bad:
They were patient and loving and full of good work.
But sadly they also had one real bad quirk:
They still worshiped idols they could not resist,
And as a result, God's blessing they missed.

Oh my ah, Oh me ah,
Oh my ah, Oh me ah,
Come see the church in Laodicea.
People there also were not very bad,
People there also were not very good;
People of Lao were just in between:
Not very friendly, yet not very mean.
They only were average—in a rut they were stuck,
So when God took one look, he simply said, "Yuk!"

These everyday Christians were not very smart;
They only loved God with a part of their heart.

Revelation 2:18-29; 3:14-22

Brother James and Brother John

Brother James and Brother John
Did everything together;
They loved the Sea of Galilee
In fair or stormy weather.

Brother James and Brother John
Cast nets upon the sea
Until Christ Jesus said one day,
"Come and follow me."

Brother James and Brother John
Tied up their boat at once;
Jesus said, "I'm Living Bread;
Let me provide your lunch."

Brother James and Brother John,
Andrew, and Simon Peter—
Twelve men in all went back to school
And Jesus was their teacher.

Brother James and Brother John
Were never once ashamed;
When their master left the earth,
His message they proclaimed.

Brother James and Brother John
Did everything together;
They freely spoke of Jesus' love
In fair or stormy weather.

Brother James and Brother John
Preached boldly home to home,
Till Herod cut off James's head
And left poor John alone.

Brother John, now by himself,
Without one hesitation,
Even though dear James was dead,
Wrote down God's Revelation.

"That's so unfair to James!" you say.
But wait, we are not done;
Now hand-in-hand with God they walk,
Brother James and Brother John.

Matthew 4:18-22
Acts 12:1-2
Revelation 1:1-2

Subject Index
People and Objects in A PILLAR OF PEPPER